LostOracle

*Ancient wisdom to find your way
in a modern world*

FIONA HORNE

ROCKPOOL

A Rockpool book
PO Box 252
Summer Hill
NSW 2130
Australia

rockpoolpublishing.com

Follow us! f 🄾 rockpoolpublishing
Tag your images with #rockpoolpublishing

ISBN: 9781922786012

Published in 2024 by Rockpool Publishing

Design and typesetting by Sara Lindberg, Rockpool Publishing
Edited by Brooke Halliwell

Printed and bound in China
10 9 8 7 6 5 4 3 2 1

Contents

Introduction

Lost Oracle emerged from my desire to offer a sanctuary, a source of solace, and a roadmap for those seeking harmony in a world often marked by chaos. In crafting this oracle, my intention is to provide a timeless guide that serves as a touchstone of reassurance, a healing balm, and a compass steering you toward success and fulfillment in all facets of your life.

Through the lens of enlightened perspectives, I hope that for you, *Lost Oracle* transforms the unknown into an enticing landscape ripe for exploration and understanding.

Steeped in ancient wisdom, *Lost Oracle* stands as your companion, helping you not only comprehend, but also navigate the complex forces surrounding and residing within you.

Lost Oracle offers timeless truths that can provide protection from persecution and confusion. It unveils a world woven with threads of hope, motivation, and liberation, holding a space where you can find refuge from morning to night.

Allow *Lost Oracle* to be your guiding light, leading you to a place where you not only seek, but truly feel found.

Using the cards

In modern times divination has retreated from the shadows of the few to be in the hands of many. Resist the urge to grab the deck and just pull a card. *Lost Oracle* encourages you to honor the sacred role that divination can play in your life and to take the time and make the effort that a sincere seeker would employ.

Storing your cards with ethically sourced crystals is beneficial as is wearing crystals or having them close by when shuffling and reading. Two of the most suitable are:

1. Moldavite – a crystal of ascension and psychic intuitive enhancement. With its origins from an ancient meteorite, it's considered to offer a pathway for wisdom from beyond this realm.
2. Amethyst – associated with the third eye chakra, it's also linked to intuition, insight and psychic abilities. Amethyst is also calming, which is a positive attribute when practicing divination to help the reader stay calm and balanced when navigating a potentially confronting landscape of feelings and impressions.

Blessing of breath

Before any divination anoint your hands with two drops of essential oil and rub gently between your palms. Cup your palms over your face, close your eyes and take three deep breaths, then place your left palm to your heart and your right to your third eye and ask for divine guidance.

Aligned oils are blue lotus, frankincense and bay leaf.

Suggested spreads

DAILY DEVOTIONAL

Altar of one

Creating a sacred ritual for your daily *Lost Oracle* card reading will infuse the practice with depth and intention. The use of the words 'devotional' and 'altar of one' offer a personalized and reverent approach.

Begin by finding a quiet and undisturbed space where you can create a sacred atmosphere. Consider dimming the lights, lighting a candle or incense, or incorporating any elements that evoke a sense of tranquility and focus.

Designate a small table or a dedicated space as your 'altar of one'. This is a sacred space that represents your personal connection to the divine and the spiritual realm. Place a special cloth or fabric on the altar to mark the territory of enlightenment.

If you have an altar stand or a specific way to hold your daily oracle card, arrange it on the altar. The stand becomes a symbolic representation of the sacred support and guidance you seek from the oracle cards. When you place your chosen card on the stand, it becomes a talisman charged with transformative energy.

Take a moment to center yourself. Close your eyes, take a few deep breaths and allow your thoughts to settle. Here is also an excellent moment to perform your 'Blessing of breath'.

Invite a sense of devotion into your space, acknowledging the sacredness of the moment and then speak to the divine, your guides or whomever you may wish to ask for help, for example:

'Sacred _____ I ask that this reading may be a portal of divine guidance in this moment, in service to myself and others.'

Think about the purpose of your daily reading. Formulate a question or set an intention for the day. This could be related to guidance, insight or simply gaining clarity on a specific aspect of your life.

With your question or intention in mind, shuffle the oracle cards. Allow your hands to move intuitively, infusing the cards with your energy and the energy of your question. When you feel ready, stop shuffling and pull one card from the deck. Place it on the altar stand, letting it become the focal point of your devotion for the day.

Open yourself to the symbolism, imagery and messages of the card. Consider how it aligns with your question or intention. Trust your intuition and the guidance that the oracle offers.

Close your daily ritual by expressing gratitude. Thank the divine, your higher self or any spiritual guides you resonated with. Acknowledge the wisdom received and carry the energy of the card with you throughout the day.

This daily oracle card ritual, with its emphasis on devotion and the altar of one, invites a sacred and personalized approach to divination. Performed regularly, it deepens your connection with the spiritual realm, provides valuable insights for your life's journey and makes it easier to absorb the lessons imparted.

THREEFOLD
Past, present, future

This threefold oracle card reading offers a holistic perspective on a specific question or situation, integrating insights from the past, present and future to provide a well-rounded understanding of the energies at play. If performing the daily altar of one, this threefold spread should only be cast twice a month.

Find a quiet and comfortable space where you won't be disturbed. Ensure that the atmosphere is conducive to reflection and focus. You may choose to light a candle, burn some incense or incorporate any elements that enhance the sacredness of the space.

Take a few moments to center yourself. Close your eyes, take a few deep breaths and allow your thoughts to settle. Here is also an excellent moment to perform your 'Blessing of breath'.

Invite a sense of devotion into your space, acknowledging the sacredness of the moment by speaking to the divine, your guides or whomever you may wish to ask for help, for example:

'Sacred _____ I ask that this reading may be a portal of divine guidance in this moment, in service to myself and others.'

Clearly articulate the question you want guidance on or set an intention for the reading. The idea is to focus the energy of the cards on a specific aspect of your life or a particular situation.

Hold the intention in your mind as you shuffle the oracle cards. Allow your intuition to guide the shuffling process, infusing the cards with the energy of your question.

Draw three cards from the deck and arrange them in a row, representing the past, present and future. Position the cards in the order you drew them, creating a sequence that flows from left to right.

- **Card 1:** represents the energies and influences of the past. Focus on how the events or energies from the past have shaped the current situation. Reflect on any lessons learned and the foundations forged that have led you to this point.

- **Card 2:** represents the present. Explore the energies and influences at play in your current circumstances. Consider how your past experiences have led to this moment and what aspects of your life are currently unfolding.

- **Card 3:** looks toward the future. It provides insight into potential developments, opportunities or challenges that may arise. Consider how the current energies and your past experiences are paving the way for future events.

'The future is created by the steps we take today.'

Fiona Horne

Explore the symbolism, imagery and messages of each card. Consider how they relate to one another and the overall narrative they create. Pay attention to any patterns, contrasts or connections between the past, present and future cards.

Think about the threefold nature of the reading. How do the past, present and future cards interconnect? What overarching themes or lessons emerge from the sequence? Allow the wisdom of the cards and any messages your guides are sending through to guide your reflections.

Close your reading by expressing gratitude for the guidance received. Whether the insights are confirming, challenging or illuminating, acknowledge the wisdom of your guides and *Lost Oracle* and carry the lessons and messages with you as you navigate the journey ahead.

THE LOST CROSS

The lost cross provides a highly structured framework that will offer you an expansive lens into layers of your being and situations contributing to your desire to do this reading.

This five-card spread should only be cast once a month.

Set the space and ask for assistance as outlined in the threefold spread.

- **Card 1:** represents the central theme or the core of the matter. It provides insight into the main focus or issue at hand. Consider this card as the heart of the reading and representative of you right now.

- **Card 2:** represents influences or energies from the spiritual realm, higher self or evolved external factors that are affecting the central theme. It can offer guidance or insights from a higher perspective.

- **Card 3:** signifies the foundation or underlying influences related to the central theme. It represents subconscious influences, past experiences or foundational aspects contributing to the current situation.

- **Card 4:** represents the past or recent influences that have led to the present situation. It offers context and background information, helping you understand the origins of the current circumstances.

- **Card 5:** provides insight into potential future developments or outcomes. It helps you anticipate what may come next or understand the trajectory of the situation.

Relationships between cards

Consider the relationships between adjacent cards. For example, how does the card above relate to the central theme? Is there a connection between the past influences (left) and the potential future (right)?

Balance and harmony

Assess the overall balance of the spread. Are the energies flowing harmoniously or do certain cards indicate conflicts or challenges? Pay attention to the overall energy and dynamics of the spread.

Card symbols and imagery

Analyze the symbols, images and any colors on each card. Look for recurring themes or contrasting elements. The imagery can provide additional layers of meaning and offer specific insights into the nuances of each position.

Intuitive impressions

Trust your intuition and initial impressions. Pay attention to any emotions, thoughts or images that come to mind, heart and body when you observe each card and its position. Your intuitive insights will add a personal and meaningful dimension to the reading.

Narrative flow

Consider the narrative flow from the past (left) to the present (center) and toward the potential future (right). How does the story unfold? Look for patterns, shifts or developments that may be indicated by the sequence of cards.

Feel free to adapt these guidelines to suit your own intuitive approach. And remember the cards are also portals for energy work. As you conduct your readings you may find corresponding shifts of energy in your body, in how you are breathing and how you are feeling. Notice these aches of acceptance and bubbles of being. They will offer further insight into your circumstances and how best to navigate them. As well as being indicators that past stored emotions are shifting, patterns are releasing and a harmonious and healed path lays ahead.

Lost Oracle

CARDS

1 • Pierce the Veil

Move beyond illusion

1 • Pierce the Veil

Move beyond illusion

The double-bladed dagger, a conduit of magick and wisdom, pierces through mists of uncertainty, reaching up into the boundless expanse of the nourishing unknown waiting to be discovered. The athame is phallic and representative of the masculine force but held in the left hand, it wields its power from the feminine perspective.

The upright triangle is the traditional witches' symbol for air in sacred magick. And the inner breeze of release can become literal when you take a deep cleansing breath while holding this card.

Embrace the revelations that come now and may challenge your current perceptions but ultimately lead to a higher understanding of your life's purpose. If you discover that something is not what you thought, do not despair, at this time it is a blessing.

Your life's journey may be confronting right now but in your hand and heart is the gift of discernment. Take another deep breath, gaze at the card, and trust your instincts and how they impact events around you.

Now is the time to focus with unwavering determination on cultivating inner strength. The element of air is your ally and as you keep your opinions to yourself and forge forward in your daily life, you minimize conflict and confrontation in your outside world.

The upright triangle also represents balance, harmony and the unification of mind, body and spirit. If you have been feeling spread thin and even somewhat torn apart, this card indicates that your pieces are now reassembling.

The balanced triangle is a reminder to nurture all aspects of your being. Take time to listen to your inner wisdom, engage in practices that nourish your physical well-being and connect with your spiritual soul through meditation and visualization. By maintaining this balance, you will find the strength and clarity needed to navigate through any ups and downs caused by the dispersal of illusions on your path. The ultimate reality you gain will be better than what you had to let go of.

2 • Harvest of the Heart

Balance strength and vulnerability

2 • Harvest of the Heart

Balance strength and vulnerability

From the battlefields of fate, a warrior emerges dressed in armor that speaks of resilience and fortitude. However, within the warrior resides a profound understanding of vulnerability, epitomized by the unguarded arm that symbolizes openness to safe and gentle interactions. This card calls upon you to reap the harvest of your fortitude, acknowledging the nourishment found in weathering storms and basking in the warmth of the sun.

The warrior's message for you now is to comprehend the divine transformation that comes by balancing guardedness with vulnerability. As a warrior in your own life, you sometimes struggle to achieve this divine balance.

If you are feeling the need to be guarded, recognize that your protective boundaries are not signs of weakness but rather manifestations of your understanding of the delicate equilibrium between trust and emotions. Be cautious of being taken advantage of, but it is important at this time to remain open to the potential of new, transformative relationships.

Past pains can sculpt a warrior who refuses to let history repeat itself. But rather than shutting everyone out, it is your journey now to discerningly close the door only to those unworthy of your trust. You now understand that trust must be earned.

Being cautious and guarded is not always a flaw, especially when navigating relationships with those who may not reciprocate your commitment and love or who are manipulative and full of trickery. When embarking on new relationships and connections, replace your guarded feelings with an awareness of the value of patience. Eventually, you will encounter someone worthy of your vulnerability. When that moment arises, consider opening your heart – but only when your company and love have been earned.

In times of earthly tribulations and inner and external conflict, cast your gaze up to the sky, for there lies your connection to the divine energy that is fuel for the wisdom of forgiveness. Take a deep breath and remember that every battle ends. That there is time and space to rest, and that you are now awakened to understanding how to navigate life's complexities with the wisdom of a warrior's heart – fortified in courage, balanced between might and vulnerability . . . and intimately connected to the flow of life's ever-turning wheel of fortune.

3 • Bounty of Happiness

This gift is for you

3 • Bounty of Happiness

This gift is for you

In a dream, you walk along a country lane at dusk. Lying in your path is a weathered wooden box with an ornate key resting in the lock. As tall, dark pines rustle and shush around you, you wonder: should you open the box?

In this pivotal moment, consider this: 'what does your intuition whisper?' Will you open it and reveal the mysteries it holds or leave it for another's dance of destiny?

Your hand reaches out and you gently grasp the key, the lock opening with a soft click. Once again you consider whether you should open it. What is holding you back?

With both hands, you raise the lid, the wood smooth and warm. Resting there in plump folds of velvet and satin a large, radiant diamond gleams.

In your life's journey, a moment of celebration beckons. Before you, a box whispers promises of treasures yet unseen. The diamond within sparkles with the brilliance of opportunity, a jewel waiting to illuminate your path.

When you stand at the crossroads of a decision, consider the key cradled in your hands and let Bounty of Happiness remind you to unlock the box and unveil the splendor it holds.

Beware of falling prey to the shadows of hesitation that would have you leave it closed for another soul to discover. The heady symphony of sacrifice may seem noble, but the music of the spheres suggests a different melody. Allow yourself to be guided toward self-compassion and the acceptance of your well-deserved rewards.

The time is ripe to cast aside the shackles of self-denial and embrace the bounty before you. The diamond, a symbol of your inner brilliance and resilience, is a gift for you to claim. Reap the rewards of your endeavors, let the light of accomplishment flood your spirit and acknowledge that this luminous treasure is rightfully yours.

The universe, in its infinite wisdom, is saying it's time to bask in the glow of your achievements and enjoy the beauty of self-affirmation this brings. It is also gently insisting on letting go of the weight of self-sacrifice. Allow yourself the indulgence of reaping the rewards of your efforts. The time for celebration is now.

Open the box and keep the diamond it contains. It is for you. This bounty of happiness is yours.

4 • Power and Might

Be free from judgment

4 • Power and Might

Be free from judgment

A simple yet powerful woman walks resolutely, carrying the nourishing fruits of harvest: a basket of apples, a pumpkin and a bundle of healing herbs. The apples are her fertile magic, cut open they reveal the sacred pentagram of seeds and the blessings of the witch.

They represent the ripe fruits of her endeavors, the mystical qualities she exudes and tangible evidence of her resilience. The healing herbs symbolize the wisdom and vitality she imparts to those willing to understand.

Beside her, a goat, the ancient lord of the forest, walks gazing up at her with trust, symbolizing a bond of understanding. It too is a creature maligned and misunderstood.

It is time to shed the false judgments that bind you. Redeem your power, for you are mightier than those who seek to diminish your light. Embrace the mystic resilience within you as your path is illuminated by the radiant glow of your authenticity.

The woman is full of might and power and it is the mysterious combination of these forces that are her birthright that shields and protects her from those who would destroy her because of their lack of these indefinable qualities.

Recognize your worth, acknowledging that the judgments of others are echoes of their reality not truths of yours. This card encourages you to cast aside the weight of misunderstanding. In doing this you can rise above the limitations imposed by others' false perceptions.

In a world of violence and harsh judgment, this card speaks of unyielding harmony. The woman is not only a healer but a living testament to the interconnectedness between humanity and the earth, her strength a force for good, a source of healing and balance in the world.

The lord of the forest, with his unwavering trust, stands as a supportive companion in her journey toward reclaiming her narrative and living in unison with the rhythms of the earth, exulting in her rightful place as a physical manifestation of the feminine divine. Like this, within you, the forces of feminine and masculine are becoming aligned and in balance.

This card speaks of resilience, empowerment, redemption and the magnification of one's strength. When you draw this card, it is time to let the world witness the unfolding of your true, unbridled power. Thank the would-be oppressors for the opportunity to unleash your intrinsic might and forge your evolving journey of self-discovery and liberation in the face of their disbelief.

5 · Found

Trust what lies ahead

5 · Found

Trust what lies ahead

A solitary woman finds solace seated on the edge of a cliff, her gaze fixed upon the setting sun and a sacred river stretching into the horizon in front of her.

In moments when life appears perplexing, this card whispers to the weary heart and says that like the ever-flowing river, the cycles of life hold mysteries that unfold under the surface. Trust that things are happening now that you do not have conscious knowledge of and that you cannot see . . . but are waiting for you just around the turn of the river bend.

Sometimes life seems complex and hard to understand. The intricate nature of your interactions, activities and very being can feel exhausting and overwhelming. The complexities of a situation tighten their hold, creating a labyrinthine dance that challenges your clarity and direction.

To unravel the complexity that surrounds you, step into the sacred waters of self-care within your home. Brew a potion of herbal teas, letting the fragrant steam envelop you, soothing away the exhaustion that clings to your spirit.

Carve out a sacred space within your dwelling and adorn it with crystals, candles and symbols that speak to you of peace and contentment. Engage in meditative dance, allowing the rhythm to synchronize with the pulse of intuitive thought.

Immerse yourself in natural surroundings and notice the intricate details of plants and flowers around you. Choose an expression of natural beauty that resonates with you, pluck a leaf or a petal, and carry it with you as a talisman.

There is a powerful message in this card for navigating relationships of the intimate kind. The setting sun, with a watchful eye, gazes at the woman who returns his look with unwavering curiosity, her hand raised to shield her eyes. In response to her presence, the sun softens his light as the earth turns.

This cosmic connection creates a harmonious dance between the polarities of masculine and feminine and a divine communion unfolds.

Embrace the alchemy of desire, the passion of lust and the warmth of love, for in their harmonious balance, a transformation begins. These energies, like fertile soil, provide the nourishment needed for embarking upon a journey of profound change. This is the moment to embrace the extraordinary and step into the richness of a life less ordinary.

6 • Celestial Queen

The stars will guide you

6 • Celestial Queen

The stars will guide you

In ancient times before light pollution of the modern era, the stars appeared to carpet the vast sky as numerous as the fibers of a heavenly rug. The footprints of a Celestial Queen were seen as she danced in the sky inviting us to join her in a dance transcending mortal boundaries – her shimmering tracks showing us the way beyond this realm.

Celestial Queen reminds you that the stars hold the shared history of humanity, connecting us through the ages, not only as we have gazed upon them, but also because we are made of them . . . we are forged from stardust.

Be prepared to experience the visions and knowledge of your ancestors and previous journeys around the sun. What lessons can you draw from the past, from the shared joy of your ancestors? Discover the threads of ecstasy woven into their stories. As you learn from the happiness of yesterday, let it guide your actions today and shape your future.

Pay attention to your astrological chart and what it is guiding you to know today. The wisdom offered in the stars is where your answers lay for the questions that you have right now. This journey of discovery can be as simple as accepting the guidance to be creative from the Celestial Queen and creating a personalized 'Astro-Intentions Vessel'.

To do this, identify your Daily Astrological Report (from your favorite online server, magazine or other reliable source), then begin your day by reading your astrological report to understand the planetary influences for that day. Identify the key areas of your life mentioned in the report, such as career, relationships or personal growth and on small pieces of paper write down specific intentions or goals related to each area. Keep these short and actionable.

Identify a box, jar or other vessel and label it as your 'Astro-Intentions Vessel'. Each intention that you have written goes into the vessel. Note: it would be appropriate to place an ethically sourced crystal into this vessel to charge your intentions. Let your intuition guide you to the crystal that resonates with you.

Throughout the day, align your activities with the themes and planetary influences mentioned in your astrological report. At the end of the day, reflect on how your activities aligned with the astrological energies. Adjust your intentions for the next day based on your reflections.

This creates a continuous and evolving cycle of intention-setting and is a mindful and intentional way to dance among the stars daily with the Celestial Queen.

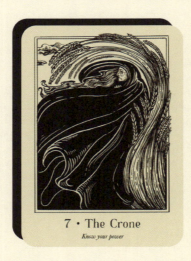

7 · The Crone

Know your power

7 · The Crone

Know your power

Here stands a beautiful wise crone, wrapped in a billowing black cloak, her hair spilling from her like ropes of silver as the winds of change embrace her. Sheaths of wheat curl around her, symbolic of her vast life's harvest and offerings.

The term crone has been burdened with negative connotations, conjuring images of haggard figures and recluses on the outskirts of society. Yet, beyond the layers of stereotype and modern insult, the true essence of the crone emerges as a powerful archetype steeped in knowledge, respect and magic.

The Crone is a paragon of wisdom and grace and embodies the culmination of a lifetime of experience. In her lies a deep well of insight, a testament to the journey that has brought her thus far.

In the feminine journey, the maiden and the crone weave a spell of intrigue and in this enigmatic card dwells the twin embodiments of womanhood, for indeed the maiden and the crone share the same throne.

When this card is drawn, you are encouraged to examine your preconceptions and assessments – are you truly self-determined? Are you embodying the wise crone's wisdom of acceptance and respect for the human journey in its many expressions?

The Crone's rightful place is also as the cornerstone of her family, the matriarch who holds the sacred knowledge of womanhood. Passing on rituals and traditions to younger generations, she is the glue that holds everything together. Are you being called to offer guidance – can you reach out a guiding hand? How is the crone resonating in you?

As you draw this card, know that much like the revered Great Mother, you are called to trust in your wisdom and knowledge. Embrace the power of self-validation and recognize the strength that comes from within. The Crone's presence assures you that the journey you've undertaken holds immeasurable value, do not doubt the choices you are making right now.

The Crone is the gatekeeper of women's mysteries and magick rooted in reality not the pages of fairytales. The magic of creation. The magic of new experiences and finding joy in the small things as we journey through the years. The life lesson of The Crone is in the reclaiming of personal power, and most importantly, *knowing* it.

8 • Disenchant

You are protected

8 • Disenchant

You are protected

In a mystical enclave where wisdom and magick reign, the ritual weaving of the Hawthorn Knot commences – a sacred dance orchestrated by the three wise crones. With reverence and intent, they pour their essence into the hawthorn tree, intertwining its branches to birth a protective knot that resonates with ancient power. In this enchanted moment, the Hawthorn Knot is born, transcending the boundaries of time and space — a living testament to the union of human wisdom, ancient cosmic forces and the magick that resides within the heart of nature.

Disenchant appears to guide you through a maze of empowerment and release. This sacred knot will shield you from unwanted energies. With it, you can stand resolute and unburdened by those who would cause you harm.

You have the power to release yourself from an unwanted admirer or lover, and the celestial forces are aligned to help you dispel false friends and vanquish psychic vampires. The full moon is a symbol of your inner radiance that can withstand even the darkest of forces, guiding you toward a reality of clarity and protection.

The hawthorn tree, revered by the Celts for its sacred properties, is deeply intertwined with the natural protective and fertility forces of the earth. The Hawthorn Knot, born from its branches, inherits this connection, it becomes a conduit for grounding and balancing energies, fostering a sense of stability and protection, while allowing the health of body, mind and spirit to prosper.

Gaze at the knot and infuse it with your intentions to assert your boundaries, protect your well-being and reclaim your sovereignty.

As you hold this card in your hand, visualize a radiant light emanating from the knot, enveloping you in a cocoon of protective energy. State an affirmation of your determining aloud, declare your sovereignty and affirm the talisman's role as a guardian of light and protector of your spirit.

Disenchant says that you are now free of the energies of naysayers and detractors and you can focus on the gifts you have to offer the world with an open heart.

9 • Beacon of Fortitude

Ground and connect

9 • Beacon of Fortitude

Ground and connect

Beacon of Fortitude is a reminder to pay attention to the practical aspects of life, such as your health, finances and home environment. It is time to ground yourself and connect with the physical world around you.

The inverted triangle of the pentacle can also represent a need to look inward and connect with your own spiritual beliefs and practices and how you express them in your everyday life. Perhaps it's time to explore new ways of connecting with the divine or to revisit old practices that have fallen by the wayside.

The triangle is formed by soft woven twigs, which encourage you to be strong but flexible as you move through the coming days. You may need to make decisions that are not easy but stay rooted in your truth yet also allow an open mind for new avenues of progress and outcomes to manifest. The sprouting tender leaves symbolize the growth and renewal that comes with being balanced between earthly and spiritual aspirations.

The man holds the pentacle up with a sense of reverence and contemplation. He is taking a moment to connect with the power of the earth and the universe, drawing strength and wisdom from the ancient symbol in his right hand which is magickally aligned with rational and logical appraisal of one's place in the world.

Whether you're seeking guidance on practical matters or spiritual growth in a logical way, Beacon of Fortitude reminds us of the importance of staying grounded and connected to the world around us as we look for alternative reasons for why events are unfolding the way they are. Resist the urge to overthink and give way to worry and obsessions.

By being emotionally intelligent and grounded as feelings swirl around, the sense of balance and harmony that results is a powerful tool for progressing forward successfully.

In the mystical realm of tarot, the pentacle suit of cards glimmers with an earthly hue, resonating with stability, grounding and abundance. This symbol of the tangible world reminds us to cherish the splendor and plenty that is available, if not in the financial realm, then in the natural world.

In the art of divination, pentacles often foretell riches and success. It is a reminder of the fruits of dedicated labor and the rewards of practicality, inviting the reader to embrace these virtues for financial security and stability. Luck is preparation meeting opportunity after all.

10 · Elixir

Your wish is granted

10 · Elixir

Your wish is granted

An open bottle, radiating an ethereal glow, contains an elixir that sparkles with untold possibilities, its magickal essence swirling in a captivating dance. Life beckons with the promise of an extraordinary adventure. The open bottle says that a journey that transcends the ordinary, offering excitement that knows no bounds and the prospect of longevity, has already commenced, now it is time to determine your direction.

To those who dare to be courageous, who possess the audacity to seize the moment and drink deeply from the elixir, great wishes shall be granted. How can you know the signs that will guide you toward the fulfillment of your best wish?

Observe the celestial dance above; look for synchronicities and signs in the heavens, as they could unveil the path illuminated by Elixir's magick.

Fear gives you the opportunity to embrace the transformative power of courage, for courage is the alchemy that turns fear into possibility. If the prospect offered by Elixir sparks a chill of fear within you, then kindle the flame of bravery and be ready to unlock the gates to your dreams.

While Elixir holds the promise of wishes fulfilled, there are considerations and warnings to heed, for every magickal journey carries both light and shadow. Ensure that your wish aligns with the truest essence of your soul. The elixir responds to authenticity and wishes rooted in the genuine desires of your heart hold the most profound power. So in this time of great potential and wishes granted think carefully. As you contemplate your wish, be still and listen to the beating of your heart – does it resonate peacefully and sustainably? Or is it a cacophony of thuds and tremors that speak of instability?

While the elixir brings the potential for greatness, temper your initial expectations. Understand that the journey may not unfold precisely as envisioned. Sometimes, Elixir's magic weaves an even grander tale, one beyond the scope of your initial wish.

Be prepared to face challenges and unknown terrains. Elixir's magic, while potent, does not shield from the inevitable ebb and flow of life. The resilience of your spirit will be your compass through storms and calms alike. Cultivate a genuine spirit of adventure within and you will learn to love life in all its light and shadow as your wish is granted.

11 • Enchantment

Use your words consciously

11 • Enchantment

Use your words consciously

Enchantment serves as a testament to the immense power of words. Speak with clarity, for the universe is closely listening. As you use your words carefully and consciously, support your efforts by surrounding yourself with sounds and visions that become your mantras – positive affirmations that echo the reality you wish to create. Let the resonance of empowering words fill your space, transforming it into a sanctuary of manifestation. Play music that inspires, listen to podcasts that uplift and hang empowering stanzas on your walls.

State this affirmation as you hold Enchantment to your heart:

'I am the weaver of my reality, crafting it with the enchanting words that flow from my being. With conscious utterance, I shape a world of my desires and surround myself with the powerful magick of positive affirmations. My words are spells, and I am the alchemist of my destiny.'

Enchantment also represents the magic and mystery of the old ways and the power that comes from connecting with ancient wisdom. The enchantments contained within this book are not just words on a page, but living energy that can transform your life if you are open to their influence. This card is an invitation to explore the secrets of the past and to connect with the power around you and within you. Trust in the magick of the universe and allow yourself to be guided by the enchantments that are flying off the pages of this spell book.

In many magickal traditions, to name is to master. This is why many witches choose a magickal name for themselves, as there is power in self-determination – and they keep their magickal name secret, revealing it only to their coven or for use in blessings and spell crafting.

Explore anchoring the guidance of Enchantment by identifying your magickal name in whatever way your intuition guides you to. Write it on parchment or dirt and bless it with ethically sourced crystals and oils. To consecrate an object of power and to align with you hold it in your left hand and state your magickal name three times.

Words will always have the power to make us feel inspired and empowered or to break down and destroy. The power of language connects us and the world, making it an integral part of our reality – practically and magickally.

12 · Encirclement

Love will flourish

12 · Encirclement

Love will flourish

Encirclement serves as a reminder that deep love and commitment when shared are a divine expression of energy. It is time to nurture your relationships with love, kindness and compassion.

This card indicates a sacred commitment will be honored to uplift, cherish and support you through life's ebbs and flows. If you are in a relationship that is challenged, then this card serves as a beacon of hope for your love to flourish and grow from a barren period. And if not the love of a romantic partner, then the love of family, friends and even co-workers come under this gentle encouragement.

As the delicate hands hold each other, the prickly thistles that frame them stand guardian, shielding this love from the outside world and those who may wish harm. In witchcraft, the thistle is considered protective and wards against curses and evil.

In the Middle Ages, the thistle was also consecrated to the Virgin Mary because its white sap suggested the milk falling from her breast for the nourishment of the Son of God. The lavender-pink color of the flower is symbolic of her divine unconditional love.

This card offers an intricate energetic dance of protection and connection as the hands are offering a gesture of reconciliation. Have you had an argument or a rift with a friend you regret? Like the pendulum, relationships swing, sometimes too far in one direction. Now is the time to allow the natural course of correction, to make space for a redefined and improved connection with one you hold dear.

Encirclement says that with openness and vulnerability, a stronger, more refined connection awaits – one that withstands the tests of time and adversity. Expressions of love in your life can grow stronger now and will when you relax your grip and gently allow your hand, whether that be physically or metaphorically, to hold another's, knowing that your love is supported and protected.

13 • Enchanted Unity

Let animals be your guides

13 • Enchanted Unity

Let animals be your guides

Unity is a powerful reminder to pay attention to the animals around you and the messages you may sense they are sending you. There are valuable insights into your physical and spiritual life and well-being being offered.

The book of spells poised above the animals is offering conjured pathways to unseen realms and secrets waiting to be revealed, as the animals gather to assist in your journey of discovery.

The broom symbolizes the power of action and transformation. It is time to sweep away obstacles and manifest your desires with purpose.

The dog represents loyalty, protection and unconditional love. This is a time to stand steadfast in your commitments and connections.

The cat reminds you to foster independence, intuition and self-reliance. Now is the time to trust your instincts and be self-sufficient even as you are loyal to others.

The raven signifies freedom and clear vision from a high perspective, encouraging you to broaden your horizons and approach life with a sense of openness and curiosity. Life is not about reaching destinations as much as comprehending that the journey itself is the destination.

The pig represents abundance, prosperity and generosity. As good tidings are bestowed on you, remember the importance of sharing your blessings with others to maintain the cosmic balance of flow and to continue your abundant state.

Together these sacred animals remind us to be playful. To be present . . . to put down the smart devices and to step out of the grind of the machine as often as possible.

Spending time with animals can have a significant positive impact on everyday well-being. Now is the time to bond with animals and accept the joy and meaning they bring to your life.

In traditional witchcraft, animals are often referred to as 'familiars', which can be spirits that take on the form of animals to help witches perform magick, or they can be animals that resonate energetically with the witch as they share a special bond, deepening her psychic, intuitive and healing abilities.

Enchanted Unity says your animal guides will help you conjure the next significant steps in your life as you cast your spell on the world.

14 • Furnace

Take action

14 • Furnace

Take action

Embrace the action of fire and burn away things that are weakening you or cluttering your path. While understanding fire's fury, embrace divine feminine wisdom of the sacred role that fire plays in our life – it warms a home's hearth and cooks food, even as it can also be a destructive force that could burn the entire house down if left unchecked.

When Furnace is drawn, it signifies that it is time for you to take action and let go of the things that are weighing you down and hindering your progress. Trust in your intuition to determine what needs to be burned away for you to move forward on your path. It is important to approach the process of release with gentle mindfulness and not extreme anger or fear.

Remember the balancing act of fire and take some time to reflect on what you truly need and what you can let go of. This may involve releasing old habits, negative thought patterns or even toxic relationships. Whatever it may be, trust that the universe has your back and that releasing these things will make room for new growth and opportunities. Visualize the flames of the fire burning away the old house as it simultaneously warms the hearth of the new.

In the sacred art of alchemy, fire is represented by the upright triangle and is the primary method used to generate a purer substance, so pure that it can fuse the material and the spiritual in the human, providing more effective benefits of integrity and clarity.

As you release what no longer serves you, allow yourself to feel lighter and more free. You are transmuting in accordance with alchemical principles.

The fire may be hot and uncomfortable at times, but the result will be worth it.

Furnace says to trust the bonfire of your life and let it warm you as it unites you with your spiritual destiny. Embrace the dance of destruction and creation, for through the flames you emerge stronger, wiser and more aligned with your true path.

15 · Gallant

Accept healing energies

15 · Gallant

Accept healing energies

When Gallant is drawn the inner masculine of your being is ready to accept healing as the masculine forces around you align to become uplifting and supportive.

Gallant represents evolved masculinity, combining the archetypal energies of king, warrior, magician and lover, without the lower expressions of domination and abuse. Instead, what flows forth from its source is empowering. The king is wise, just and creative. The warrior offers the energy of assertive action. The magician offers transformation, while the lover enables connection to the world in a dynamic and outgoing way.

When these archetypes combine it is a potent force and this card heralds a time of healing and acceptance for the masculine aspects of your being aiding you to shed the weight of past traumatic experiences.

Take comfort in knowing that you are not alone in your healing journey. The universe is conspiring to bring you the support and guidance that you need as long as you stay open and receptive to this energy. Accept offers of help and gestures of kindness from the masculine around you. Remember to be kind and gentle with yourself too as trauma-based resistance may build and confront you before shifting.

Remember that the divine masculine is not just about strength and power, but also about compassion and nurturing. As you embrace this energy, you will find that your relationships are more balanced and strengthened, and your sense of self-worth is deepened.

As energies align the guidance of the divine masculine may come in unexpected ways. It could be through a conversation with a friend, a sign from nature or a sudden realization that seems to appear out of nowhere but is a symptom of your internal psychic shift. Stay open and receptive to these messages and trust that they are leading you toward your highest good, even if you feel vulnerable.

As the divine masculine shines its light around you, remember there is a corresponding light shining within you too. You now have the power to be strong, compassionate and nurturing toward yourself and others. Allow this energy to flow through you and its light to guide you toward your most evolved purpose.

Under the influence of this evolved masculine energy relationships that were once strained begin to mend. As past traumas fade, a sense of resilience and optimism prevails.

16 • Green Man

It's time to grow

16 • Green Man

It's time to grow

The Green Man is a pagan symbol who encompasses the cycles of life, death and rebirth. He is representative of divine masculinity (God) and that active place where this combines with the omniscient presence of the divine feminine (Goddess).

The Green Man is born in spring and heralds the return of abundant crops and growth on the land. He is a guardian of the earth and a male energy that can be trusted to bring dynamic positive change and new nourishing opportunities of love.

While there is an eeriness to his presence as he emerges from the darkness, be aware that his eyes glow with the light of the life-giving sun. His darkness is lush and fertile, and he teaches that the dark times in your life are essential for the cyclical balance to allow growth and abundance, and encourages observation of these natural cycles to soothe and calm an anxious heart and mind caught up in fears of lack and loss.

The Green Man says to open your heart to the blessings he brings and embrace the lush vegetation of possibilities that are unfolding before you. His essence assures you that positive transformations are underway, and with trust and faith you will experience a new season of growth, love and bountiful opportunities.

This card is a reminder that while you may have experienced pain and trauma at the hands of men, there are also positive and healing aspects of masculinity that can support and empower you. Allow yourself to be open to these energies and embrace the opportunities for growth and renewal that are available to you now.

Like Mother Earth, the Green Man also represents a deep connection to the earth, reminding you to spend time in nature and connect with the natural world around you. By doing so, you can ground yourself and find peace and clarity amid any chaos or uncertainty.

The Green Man's message is a powerful one: he is a symbol of the re-emergence of the sacred masculine presence whose balance shall be righted in the modern world, and a symbol of hope and renewal, especially during times when we may feel stuck or stagnant. By embracing the cycles of life and death, we can learn to trust in the process of dynamic change and transformation.

17 · The Stang

Ride between the realms

17 · The Stang

Ride between the realms

The Stang is a forked staff that channels the primal
and powerful energies of the old ways of witchcraft.
It serves as a bridge between worlds, symbolically used
to 'ride' between the realms of existence, is a symbol

of the Horned God, and a tool for directing energy toward deep transformation.

The masculine has been debased in modern society to become something that is not sustainable – when the wise crone rides the stang she helps guide the masculine home again to a place of deep purpose and place – where strength is constructive and used to help and hold up and not destroy.

Like the wise crone, you too have the power to navigate the patriarchal world's conflicting messages and challenging detours with grace, purpose and a deep connection to the pure primal forces that shape sustainable existence.

When you draw this card it is an invitation to bridge the masculine and feminine and gain deeper insight into your life's purpose. The wise crone steps off and hands you the stang – what do you feel drawn to doing? To wield it over your head like a potent powerful staff of magick and conjure a new reality? Or climb atop it to ride between the realms and gain guidance as to what that new reality could or should be?

In ancient traditions and spiritual practices, the masculine was revered for its ability to provide direction, protection and support. The Stang is a symbol of this masculine energy and by reclaiming its positive aspects we can create a more balanced and harmonious world. We can learn to use our strength and power in ways that are constructive and supportive, and we can work together to create a society that values compassion, kindness and understanding.

The Stang is a reminder that nature is a sacred conduit, a bridge to the spirit world and your ancestors wish to guide you. In the realm of sleep the boundaries between worlds blur, and the subconscious becomes a canvas upon which they paint visions and symbols laden with significance. Keep a dream journal and record these visions and symbols. They will be useful keys to unlock the mysteries of your path.

It is important to note that in this modern age the masculine and feminine energies are not limited to gender identities. Everyone has access to both energies and can embody them in different and unique ways. By understanding and respecting these energies and how they manifest in the modern human, we can create a more accepting and compassionate world for all.

18 · Hand of Fire

Stoke your inner flame

18 · Hand of Fire

Stoke your inner flame

Hand of Fire is a powerful symbol of transformation and passion. It represents the energy and drive that you possess to achieve your goals and make your desires a reality. When you draw this card, it is reassurance that you have the power to create the life you passionately desire and that you should stoke your inner fire with confidence and let it light your life's path.

Have you been neglecting your passions or holding back due to fear or self-doubt? The flames on the fingertips are a reminder to let go of inhibitions and allow your true desires to guide your choices and actions. Do those things you couldn't and stop doing the things that don't make you happy or feel authentically expressed.

Fire is the most dynamic element of change and energies around you align now to aid you in manifesting your dreams and making things happen, even if you feel your efforts have fallen short before. Trust in your abilities and let your passion fuel your success as your ideas and dreams have the potential to create something truly extraordinary, both in the lives of others and your own.

The flames symbolize the intensity and drive needed to manifest your visions into reality. Let their sacred heat remind you to approach your goals with enthusiasm, determination and a willingness to take risks.

The Hand of Fire warns you to use your fire wisely and ethically. As your passion fires up treat everyone with respect and support even as your own light may eclipse theirs. The people you meet on the way up are also the people you meet on the way down. Everything good and bad has a beginning, a middle and an end. Remember when great success and acclaim are achieved to acknowledge all that helped you reach this place of exultation. The Hand of Fire says to stay grounded and grateful.

Remember, the fire on your fingertips now is a gift. Use it wisely, harness its energy and let it guide you toward a future filled with purpose, fulfillment and the realization of your dreams. And then you truly shall create positive change in your life and the world around you.

19 • Harvest Ritual

Trust the endings in life

19 • Harvest Ritual

Trust the endings in life

The skeleton represents the long sleep of death and the transition from one form of existence to another. The pumpkins are a symbol of the harvest, of a life well-lived and it is now time to acknowledge all your efforts that have reaped rewards . . . and also those that did not turn out the way you expected.

Trust the little deaths and the endings in your life, because they have sweet and hearty sustenance that can feed not only you but the events, circumstances and relationships that will live on in your life. It's important to remember that the endings we experience are not always negative. Sometimes, they are necessary for our growth and development. By letting go of the past, we can make room for new opportunities and experiences that will help us evolve and thrive.

A good life and a good death are threads intricately woven together. Recognizing death as an essential component of appreciating life is a profound perspective that can enrich our understanding of the human experience.

Take a moment to reflect on your mortality. Rather than evoking fear, this contemplation can serve as a catalyst for a more intentional and meaningful life. Recognizing the finiteness of our time urges us to prioritize what truly matters, fostering a sense of purpose and forgiveness for the times when life was less than perfect.

The Japanese concept, *Mono no aware*, recognizes the beauty of transience. Find appreciation in the fleeting nature of cherry blossoms, the changing seasons or the setting sun. Just as nature gracefully transitions, so do our lives.

Understand that loss, though often painful, is an integral part of the human experience. Grief, when embraced as a natural response to loss, can become a teacher. Through mourning, we learn to appreciate the essence of what was lost and find strength in the process of healing.

Harness the awareness of life's impermanence to live with intention. Align your actions with your values and aspirations. Channel the awareness of mortality into a drive to create a positive legacy. Whether through meaningful relationships, contributions to society or personal achievements, your legacy is a testament to a life well-lived.

And one day you can lay like the smiling skeleton at peace surrounded by the nourishing harvest of your wonderful life. And as the snake coiled at the base suggests, you can be reborn into the next.

20 • Hearth

Broaden your horizons

20 • Hearth

Broaden your horizons

When Hearth appears a new dwelling beckons,
not merely a physical abode, but a sanctuary of
the soul. Hearth whispers its timeless truths of the
need to sometimes retreat from the world to a safe

nourishing space . . . but does this have to be the same space forever?

Where would you be if not where you are now? Reflect on the sacred element of time and evolution. The hermit crab carries her home on her back, the borrowed shell a vessel of continuity. When she grows out of it she lets go and finds another shell, allowing her to adapt to new environments as she grows and evolves. We too must be willing to shed the remnants of the life we have lived and embrace the journey of personal evolution – new homes and new lives.

Embrace the warmth offered by Hearth, for within these walls you find not just shelter but a cocoon for transformation. The empty bag hanging by the door signifies potential and the call to explore new horizons. As you stand at the cottage door, poised between the familiar and the unknown, let Hearth reassure you. Open the door with anticipation, for beyond it lies sparkling webs of possibility, and within it resides the alchemy of your personal magick.

Remember that the journey toward personal growth and transformation is not always easy, and it requires a willingness to step out of your comfort zone and embrace the unknown. But by doing so, you will discover new aspects of yourself that you never knew existed and experience a sense of fulfillment and purpose that comes from living a life that is true to your evolving values and passions.

Meditate on the image of the Hearth card and its powerful pentagram etched into its door, and let it serve as a reminder to nurture your inner flame, anchor your dreams in the physical realm and create a life that is both beautiful and meaningful.

The black cat is a witch's familiar and psychic guide. Its presence illuminates the shadows, and you can take comfort in knowing you are not alone in your journey.

The broom is a special witch's broom, its role is to sweep away unwanted energies. It guards your sacred space, creating a barrier against unwelcome visitors, both mundane and metaphysical.

Embrace the magick of Hearth for in this enchanted haven, you are not just a dweller but the alchemist of your destiny.

21 · House of Love

You shall be loved

21 · House of Love

You shall be loved

The power is in your hands to conjure the love you seek – like the sorceress in the House of Love, you are now the designer of love's destiny.

In a sacred space flooded with incantations, she weaves together a bouquet of sacred herbs and blossoms, crafting a love charm that resonates with the symphony of your heart. Her magick is for you. In this moment you become a beacon of light set forth in the dark night of creation's cauldron, a shining star for the one who loves you to follow.

You are not merely the seeker now, but the sought. Be seen by the one who loves you, as this magick becomes a radiant force drawing love into your life and the energy of your life's love spell echoes in the cosmos, creating a harmonious vibration that resonates with the heart of another.

Your thoughts are threads and with them you are weaving your romantic destiny.

Love magick, a dance of energies, extends out beyond the realm of external connections and back inwards to its source, which is the most potent magick – self-love. The cauldron of creation within is stirred by whispers of self-affirmation and acceptance.

The sacred herbs and blossoms within the House of Love symbolize the nurturing of your own garden, the cultivation of self-love. Wear colors and anoint yourself with scents chosen to please you and are a celebration of your uniqueness, a recognition of your worthiness of love in all its forms.

Now you are not just the one who is sought by others, but you are the one who seeks oneself with love and compassion.

Casting love spells is a sacred act with special laws and rules, but the House of Love offers that this spell is cast for you for the good of all with harm to none. Honoring all emotional laws and spiritual regulations. Let its magick work in your life. Be bright, be blessed. You are loved.

22 · Lost

Choose joy as your compass

22 · Lost

Choose joy as your compass

In Lost a girl stands at the threshold of discovery, her red locks brimming with the fertile energy of possibility as she gazes into the pregnant dark of the ancient grove of trees stretching out before her.

Unbeknown to her, a magnificent castle awaits atop a distant mountain – its presence hidden beyond her current vantage point. Her pure curiosity and willingness to step into the unknown will be rewarded when she discovers the grand beauty and comfort that awaits her discovery.

In her mind, a mantra repeats: 'I am so excited for my future; I could see the most incredible things, meet the most wonderful people and have the most remarkable adventures.'

A sense of joy and anticipation suffuses her – her only duty is to cultivate these feelings.

It is time for you to choose to explore a new place that calls to your soul, even if the path ahead seems obscured by shadows. Let the fear that tugs at your heart transform into flickers of excitement, the delicious anticipation of what lies beyond the familiar.

As you traverse the unknown, remember that the journey itself is a teacher. Each step, each moment of uncertainty is a note in the song of your growth. You will hear the call of the castle on the mountain, symbolic of your aspirations, growing louder with every fearless stride. Let this knowledge put a smile on your face.

This is not only a physical exploration but a pilgrimage of the soul. Trust that the courage to take the first step is a gift to yourself and a beacon for those who are destined to walk beside you.

In the realm of magick, the name Lost encapsulates the essence of this journey – 'all who wander are not lost' but are taking a delightful and joyful sojourn into the unknown – and while this indicates great new developments, it is also a reminder to take these a day at a time.

As you stand at the threshold not lost, but armed with thrilling excitement and a sense of joy for your upcoming adventure, know that the very act of choosing joy as your compass opens the door to great mysteries that will enrich the rest of your life. Revealing not only the mysteries of the external world but also illuminating the fascinating sacred landscapes within you.

23 · Blessed Resilience

You can weather the storm

23 · Blessed Resilience

You can weather the storm

In the year 1683, amid the shadows of suspicion and fear, a woman named Mary Webster found herself accused of witchcraft. A trial unfolded and against the odds, she was declared not guilty. Yet, the story did not end there.

In 1684, the verbal accusations persisted, this time from Philip Smith – a judge, a deacon, a representative of Hadley, where Mary and her husband lived. His misguided beliefs led to a dark experiment, a testament to the superstitions that gripped the minds of the time.

As Smith lay afflicted, a group of young men, in their ignorance and cruelty, subjected Mary Webster to a harrowing ordeal. They took her from her small home, hung her, rolled her in the snow and finally buried her in it, leaving her for dead. But Mary's spirit, indomitable in the face of adversity, survived. And the man who accused her happened to die.

Blessed Resilience bears witness to Mary Webster's resilience – in this terrible and sad story she is a symbol of triumph over injustice, her strength of spirit that defied the stupidity of youth and the darkest aspect of the patriarchy available to you. When this card is drawn, it carries a message of enduring through misfortune and overcoming misjudgment – those who have wrongly accused you will meet their own judgment in the eyes of the divine.

Goodness will prevail in your favor, and you too can weather the storms of life. This card is a beacon of hope, a testament to the enduring power of the human spirit. In times of challenge, hold onto the knowledge that, like Mary Webster, you will emerge from the snow, not buried by it, but strengthened and transformed by your resilience.

In her heart, Mary carries the wisdom echoed in the compassionate words of Jesus on the cross: 'Forgive them, Lord, for they know not what they do.' Despite the brutality inflicted upon her, she understands that the cruelty comes from a place of ignorance.

The power of forgiveness and compassion is immense. It not only frees the person who forgives, but it also can transform the oppressor.

The broomstick beneath Mary symbolizes not only escape but also transcendence – the ability to rise above the pettiness and cruelty of others, as Mary gently hugs the little black cat to her chest. This gesture is a powerful reminder to extend gentleness and kindness even to those who oppress you for then you are truly free and the victor.

24 • Primordial Passion

Leave your mark

24 • Primordial Passion

Leave your mark

When Primordial Passion appears it is time to tap into the deep wellspring of the primal origins of the human condition and put down the electronics, eschew the AI and all associated facilitators that are supposed to enhance our efforts, and which are in fact, dulling our creative human spirit. Instead, create a work of living art that reflects your organic origins.

Others may dismiss your efforts because they seem archaic and outdated – but you will win the naysayers over to your methods. As the woman in the image uses her hands to communicate her creative truth, so too can you use your words and actions to win over those who may doubt you. Your ability to enchant and empower others now is a formidable tool. And in doing so you can expect success in your endeavors.

Be generous, be wise, be bold and kind . . . and no one will refuse you. These qualities create an irresistible aura. When you embody these virtues, everything you do will be seen as entrancing and desirable.

This is the card of the artist but if you are not an avowed artist, fear not – all creations are art – whether it is the display of food on a plate, the way a scarf is added to a garment, a smile that is offered to a stranger and changing the appearance of their day. Or even the smile you offer yourself in the mirror that changes the appearance of your day. Every act of creation is art and these acts are not mere embellishments, they are sacred offerings that touch the hearts of those who encounter them.

In the realm of sacred geometry, the spiral is a fundamental pattern. It is often linked to the Fibonacci sequence, a mathematical progression found in nature's designs. This connection imbues the spiral with a sense of divine order, harmony and balance in the cosmos – from its primal origins . . . out into the universe . . . and back again.

As the woman crouches in front of the standing stone her visceral efforts of creation primal and pure, she focuses and magnifies the meaning and purpose of her existence . . . cocreating and leaving her mark on the world.

25 • Midnight Brew

The alchemy of you

25 • Midnight Brew

The alchemy of you

The Midnight Brew card emerges as a symbol of transformation and the potent energies of change. The cauldron, a vessel of ancient magic, represents the crucible of your life experiences and the potential for profound alchemy.

The potion bubbling over signifies the release of hidden potential, untapped wisdom and creative energies. Your life is in a state of flux and powerful forces are at work, bringing forth opportunities for growth and renewal. Embrace the transformation that is underway as the burning wood beneath the cauldron represents the purifying fires of change. Just as fire transforms wood into ash, your challenges are catalysts for your evolution.

The owl, a creature of the night, perches on the cauldron's lid as a guardian of ancient wisdom. In the darkness, profound insights are revealed. The owl invites you to explore the hidden realms of your subconscious where profound truths and ancient knowledge reside. The alchemical process may not always be comfortable, but it is a necessary step toward personal and spiritual growth.

Most significantly, the owl represents fascinating silence. They are creatures of aerial stealth. Due to their unique feather structure, they fly without a sound. In this time of midnight brewing of your potential, the owl tells you to be silent. To not brag or boast, to not draw attention to the magick that is bubbling inside you. Silence through the preparation of your alchemical brew will give you a useful advantage.

In mythology, the cauldron is a symbol of rebirth and regeneration. It is said that the Welsh goddess

Cerridwen enchanted a cauldron of transfiguration to brew a potion that granted beauty, wisdom and poetic inspiration. The outcome of this time will surprise and inspire you as its full magickal potential is released.

As the cauldron bubbles at midnight know that one version of you is ending . . . and the next enchanted one, is beginning.

26 · Nascent

Your potential is ripe

26 · Nascent

Your potential is ripe

Nascent heralds the emergence of an opportunity that has been quietly growing, nurtured by the seeds of the past. This is a moment of realization: your future potential is rapidly ripening. The time has come to review the plans you once set in motion and reflect on the dreams and hopes that seemed to yield no fruit. You were not patient enough to know then what you can know now.

The red ladder against the tree symbolizes your willingness to take proactive steps toward your aspirations. Revisit your goals with fresh eyes and an open heart.

Trust again in something or someone you once believed in, for they may now hold the key to the promise you seek. Life's seasons bring cycles of growth, and what may have seemed dormant is now ripe for harvest. The apples on the top boughs represent the tangible rewards of your efforts, relationships that have evolved and things that were 'before their time' are now perfectly timed and aligned. These fruits are dangling within reach.

Hold Nascent to your heart, close your eyes and consider the abundance of possibilities and potential outcomes from all variables of your life. Visualize the fruits of your labor, both seen and unseen, and understand that your tree carries the essence of your aspirations.

See them now, reach up and pluck your fruits from the branch – they are rightfully yours.

This is a card that says 'Yes'.

Yes, to a new opportunity, yes to an offer, yes to love, yes to the past, yes to the future.

Consider your journey not as a series of isolated rungs to climb, but as an interconnected network of ladders leading to various aspects of your life. Each rung is an opportunity to learn, evolve and reach higher states of understanding. Life is dynamic and Nascent urges you to approach each step with vitality and a zest for the burgeoning possibilities that lie ahead.

So, as you stand beneath the tree of your life with your red ladder, take a moment to appreciate the miraculous fecundity of your life's landscape. Acknowledge the achievements of the past that fertilize your future as you gaze upward with anticipation for the new heights waiting to be conquered, and new fruits waiting there, ripe for the plucking.

27 · Naivete

Cultivate innocence

27 · Naivete

Cultivate innocence

Naivete beckons you to embrace qualities of sincerity, unpretentiousness and trustfulness in a world often saturated with hubris. The woman on the cliff reaching over to pluck a ripe flower epitomizes the spirit of naivete, a willingness to reach toward something beautiful with innocence and trust.

In a society where narcissism flows like tap water, naivete with its innocence and lack of jaded perspective becomes the antidote to a self-centered and exhausted world and can offer a fresh and genuine perspective of life.

Foster the purity of your intentions as you embody the spirit of Naivete. Allow yourself to trust with an open heart, knowing that the genuine connections you desire are built on a foundation of trust. Discard preconceived notions and old fears.

Naivete parallels the concept of The Fool in the Tarot, representing the innate trusting element within us. As he stands on the edge of a cliff about to leap, he cries out, 'Catch me, universe, I'm looking forward to seeing where I land!' This confidence of spirit empowers us to take leaps of faith into the world, transforming not only our lives but also the lives of others. It becomes a force to elevate the human condition, reminding us that in the pursuit of beauty and goodness, a certain level of naivete is a powerful catalyst for positive change.

In a world where skepticism often prevails, the woman's certitude is not a reckless abandon but a deep understanding that the universe responds to authenticity and sincerity. As she leans over the cliff, she is connected to a cosmic flow, a force that recognizes and supports genuine intentions. Her trust is a profound acknowledgment that the universe is a benevolent force, and by aligning herself with its currents, she opens herself to the guidance and protection it provides.

Naivete is a reminder that sometimes the most profound beauty and gifts of existence lie just beyond the edge of our comfort zone, waiting to be embraced by those who dare to trust and cultivate their innocence, and remaining open to all opportunities to find out not what they can't do . . . but what they *can*.

28 · Papillon

Your courage will be rewarded

28 · Papillon

Your courage will be rewarded

The butterflies with their delicate but strong wings, born of the dark yet nourishing constraints of their cocoons, symbolize the magic of tenacity, transformation and renewal. Papillon heralds the journey of rebirth, both within oneself and in the realm of the spirit. It is time to shed the cocoon of the past and emerge in a new form, embodying the essence of authentic selfhood.

The butterflies' escape from the thorn-filled jar heralds liberation from painful constraints. Their flight urges you to venture forth into the uncharted; your fearlessness will be rewarded. If a situation or person has been holding you back and causing pain and grief, Papillon says it is time now for you to fly free, and your struggle will have yielded important personal growth.

Poppies tell tales of sleep, the cycle of life and death, peace and the eternal dance of rebirth. They are a metaphorical bridge between the waking world and the afterlife, with their presence symbolizing the delicate and transient nature of existence. With their vibrant and delicate petals, poppies often carry dual meanings. On one hand, they are associated with beauty, passion and the ephemeral nature of life.

Yet, the poppy also has a darker side, as it has historically been linked to the concept of remembrance and the sacrifices made during times of war. The trauma and sensory overload of war are contrasted with the poppy's relationship to the opium dens of romantic literature.

Papillon is also the card aligned with awareness of addictions and their ultimately unsustainable role in human life. The butterflies represent freedom from the constraints of drugs, food, relationships and physical/emotional addictions.

The juxtaposition of beauty and solemnity in the poppy's symbolism speaks to the complex nature of the human experience. It reminds us that even in moments of joy and vibrancy, there may be underlying challenges or sacrifices. This does not mean that life is hard, or we have failed.

The message of Papillon offers that on the path of transformation and enlightenment, one may encounter both the soft allure of ease and beauty and the sharp prick of challenges. The jar, as a symbol of containment, suggests that these elements coexist and contribute to the richness of the journey.

Embracing the navigation between both the poppies and the thorns allows for a more profound understanding of the self and a greater appreciation for the complexities inherent in the process of personal metamorphosis. And when it is time and you have contemplated the challenges with compassion, fly free and leave them behind.

29 · Phenomenon

Expect the extraordinary

Phenomenon says the extraordinary is within reach. Illuminate your inner self. Reflect your passions, ignite your determination and let the fusion of intuition and will guide your actions. Embrace the moon's reflective wisdom and the sun's bold radiance within.

The skyclad woman, her hands reaching up and touching the moon, her eyes closed in bliss, is trusting and happy, she feels valued and free. She has learned many lessons and one of them is the sacred ancient ritual called 'Drawing Down the Moon'. The secret to this powerful transference of lunar energy is that as she receives, her body fueled with her intention becomes a portal that magnifies the energy back out into the cosmos. Because her greatest power is measured not by what she gets, but by what she is empowered to give. And balanced between receiving and giving she becomes a magnet for success in all things.

The ancient stone archway is one of the portals of quantum possibilities. Arches, when first created 3000 years ago, were considered gateways to the divine. Passing through an archway symbolized a transition from the mundane to the sacred – and in your life now there is an opportunity to step through. Make the decision now and trust your choice – it is supported.

This card heralds a time of unfettered creativity and unconventional problem-solving. Embrace the unexpected, challenge assumptions and let your unique perspective be the guiding light in the labyrinth of your existence.

The moon above the woman is no static orb; it's a living key, a bridge between realms. As you draw the moon into yourself, unexpected revelations flow – an infusion of celestial energies awakening latent powers within. Commune with your lunar self – meditate, spend time in solitude, explore your shadow and embrace your mysteries. The unexpected lies in the depth of this self-discovery.

Embrace the quirks, talents and idiosyncrasies that set you apart. Find your brilliance in the fusion of your distinct, unique experiences and perspectives.

To assist in unleashing your brilliance, create a cosmic vision board that reflects your dreams and aspirations. Use it as a visual reminder of your extraordinary potential and the path you're forging.

Craft written and spoken affirmations that attest to your unique brilliance, expressing confidence in your abilities and your journey toward becoming a phenomenon. When you experience yourself as a phenomenon, the world around you will too.

30 · Raconteur

You are the catalyst

30 · Raconteur

You are the catalyst

The woman of Raconteur is a shapeshifter – she can turn even mundane experiences into invigorating and extraordinary exploits. Her head thrown back, she drinks from the book of magick enchanting others with her presence, as its contents imbue her with mystical knowledge and powers. Like her, now is the time for your heightened intuition and getting of wisdom. The magick within you cannot be contained.

Don't wait for the world to change around you – you are the catalyst; you are the change that is needed. Transform yourself and the world will be different.

It is time for you to be an inspirer, an exciter, a catalyst for positive change. In the grand theater of life, you are now the entertainer, engaging the imaginations of those around you with the sheer brilliance of your spirit. Through your zest for life, you have the power to uplift and transform. And if you are not feeling this way right now, Raconteur says you are stepping into a period where you will on every level – whether that be spiritual or physical – in relationships, work and all human endeavors. This is not a finite exercise or brief transitory moment in your life – it is the rest of your life.

As the animals of Raconteur all leap at the woman's feet offering their qualities for her efforts, they offer themselves now to you.

When you shapeshift as the fox, you embody the clever and adaptable spirit of this magickal creature. Resourcefulness and quick thinking is now available to you and you hold the ability to move gracefully between different realms of understanding, uncovering hidden truths and embracing the power of adaptability.

Shapeshifting into the form of an owl brings the wisdom of the night and the ability to see beyond the surface. Your intuition is heightened and you become a harbinger of insight and knowledge.

When you shapeshift to the hare, you are now quick and nimble, leaping fearlessly into the unknown. You bring fertility to ideas and projects, cultivating a sense of abundance and growth.

Shapeshifting into a cat unveils your mysterious and independent nature. Cats are creatures of both grace and ferocity and in this form, you possess the ability to move between worlds effortlessly and independently.

As you navigate the realms of shapeshifting, like the woman of Raconteur, know that the world is your enchanted playground and you bring a sparkle of magick to every corner. And as you transform you will experience a corresponding elevation in the circumstances of your life.

31 · Spiral

Time for rest and repose

31 · Spiral

Time for rest and repose

Life is never perfect, but perseverance can get us through challenges that seem insurmountable. Spirals of doubt can be transfigured into spirals of inspiration. Twist and twirl, retrace and flow – you are not grinding your path but forging and expanding it with sinuous strength now. You can see past your current predicament and move on in your life with courage and determination. But Spiral says, first you must rest.

In the symbolism of the serpent, you are connected to the ancient Great Goddess, a powerful force that transcends time. The snake, with its shedding of skin, embodies the eternal cycle of life, death and rebirth – an eternal dance of transformation.

In the same way, the serpent, unburdened by the ticking clock, epitomizes the freedom of timeless existence. As you gather your strength in the coil of contemplation, liberate yourself from constraints of urgency. Take all the time you need, for time, after all, is a construct crafted by humanity for social convenience.

The easeful, muscular coil of the snake invites you to luxuriate in rest, repose and recalibration. Let this period of stillness be a sensuous interlude – a time to gather the energy needed for the next strike at life's opportunities. The snake, in its wisdom, knows that readiness to strike is born from a tranquil mind and a rejuvenated spirit. In this serenity find the power to shed old skin, release unnecessary burdens and emerge renewed and revitalized.

Trust that your period of stillness will be fertile ground for growth, and with your hunger for life awakened, you will strike at the next opportunity fresh, empowered, invigorated and aligned with what is best for you.

32 • Ancestral Alchemy

Conjure your legacy

32 • Ancestral Alchemy

Conjure your legacy

Ancestral Alchemy witnesses moonlight meeting shadows as sacred transmissions between the living and the departed unfold. The woman engages in a ritual to communicate with her ancestors, and she invites you to recognize the importance of acknowledging and venerating death. In some cultures, death is seen as a grand adventure, a transition rather than an end. It is revered, respected and integrated into the natural flow of existence.

In modern western society, where consumerism often shapes values, death is frequently feared and avoided. The quest for eternal life has led to perceiving death as an 'illness' to be treated, a condition to be conquered. Consider the implications this has on the human condition – what is lost when the inevitability of death is denied?

Ancestral Alchemy serves as an invitation to walk alongside your ancestors, recognizing their influence and wisdom that echoes through time . . . and through you.

Engage in your own ritual of remembrance. Speak to your ancestors, ask questions and offer them reverence. In doing so, you integrate their stories into your own, creating a mosaic of moments that spans generations. The wisdom of those who came before can guide you, illuminating the path forward with insights drawn from the vast reservoir of their collective experience.

The ring of skulls symbolizes not just the end of life but also the enduring spirit that transcends physical form. Your ancestors faced challenges, overcame obstacles and left behind a legacy of resilience. In acknowledging their strength, you tap into a well of courage that resides within you. Death, in this context, becomes a testament to the endurance of the human spirit and attests that your actions, choices and the way you navigate life contribute to the ongoing narrative of your lineage.

Ancestral Alchemy represents a sacred calling, a mystical and enchanting responsibility to spiritually safeguard the future of your bloodline. You may like to sanctify this calling with a ritual of your own creation. Trust that your intentions and the power of ancient magick will bring appropriate good fortune to your family's bloodline for generations to come.

33 • Stardust and Soil

Opposites attract

33 • Stardust and Soil

Opposites attract

The left hand that reaches through the Ouroboros is yours . . . and it reveals the profound truth that you are not merely a physical being navigating the material world, you are a spiritual entity having a temporary physical experience. As your ethereal fingers touch the flowering plant, the celestial and earthly unite in beauty – a harmonious expression of your dual nature.

The Ouroboros, an ancient symbol of eternity, invites contemplation on the interplay between the temporal and the eternal. Your journey through cycles of growth, decay and rebirth reflects this dance of stardust and soil.

Spirit and physical are opposites that attract and exist as witnesses to each other. Stardust and Soil thus speaks to human relationships and offers that successful relationships can be forged between individuals who may seem completely incompatible. The key lies in recognizing, respecting and embracing the inherent differences while co-existing to create a harmonious and transformative union, both in the physical realm and in the soulful space.

In alchemy, the Ouroboros represents the unity of opposites and is deeply tied to the philosophical and spiritual pursuits of the alchemists. As a symbol of wholeness, it also suggests that the union of opposites completes a circle. Similarly, in a successful relationship, the coming together of two individuals with diverse qualities can create a sense of completeness and fulfillment. In a relationship that transcends the physical, two individuals complement and support each other's spiritual growth.

Now is the time to examine your relationships and determine where friction can be useful and acceptance of differences empowering. Trust these differences that nurture your relationships, whether romantic, friendships, family or workmates.

This oracle card speaks to your role as a conscious co-creator of your reality. The flowering plant and its journey from seed, to bud, to blossom, to seed, symbolizes the tangible outcomes of your intentions, highlighting the potency of your thoughts, emotions and actions in sculpting your journey. Know this wisdom and see where you can trust differences around you and let your life proceed more harmoniously.

34 • Under Siege

Uproot your habits

34 • Under Siege

Uproot your habits

All your enemies lie within. Mental health struggles under a siege of habits. Deep laid patterns of thought are hard to uproot but uprooted they must be; therefore, tear out the invading thoughts of loss and strife without hesitation. Lay bare the field to expose your enemies and fight a fair battle *with yourself.* Victory is yours.

The woman in the image is wearing an expression of despair and sadness, finding herself confined underground within a fortress of intertwined roots. The hole she dug to plant new dreams now encapsulates her in a self-made prison. This is the emotional hole we sometimes unintentionally dig, trapping our spirits in a dark sensation of self-imposed limitations.

Under Siege invites you to acknowledge the walls you've unintentionally built. By recognizing these self-imposed limitations, you reclaim the power to dismantle them. In this acknowledgment lies the key to your emotional freedom.

As you consider the hole that you are in, treat yourself with compassion. Under Siege is an invitation to be gentle with your inner struggles. Understand that the fortresses were built as a form of self-protection and embrace the opportunity for self-healing and self-love as you dismantle these old barriers.

The fortress may seem formidable, but it is an illusion. Just as it was built, it can be dismantled. Just as the hole was dug, it can be climbed out of and filled. (In fact, the tangle of roots is a ladder for your ascent.)

Look up . . . and you will see the sunlight.

Under Siege recognizes the allure of depressive thoughts – a dark and, at times, strangely delightful addiction. The familiarity of sadness can become a comfort, a well-worn path that the mind retreats to. This card invites you to acknowledge the addictive nature of these thoughts and understand that, while they may offer temporary solace, they are not sustainable sources of strength.

This card presents an opportunity for profound transformation. The battle against inner foes is not just a struggle but a chance to redefine patterns of addiction in life.

By looking up and climbing into the light, you not only free yourself from the siege within but also harness the energy to redefine your life, turning challenges into opportunities for growth, creativity and lasting well-being.

35 • Unguarded

Trust the unexpected

35 • Unguarded

Trust the unexpected

The woman lies on the back of a huge female bear.
She is relaxed and comfortable as the bear carries her
with gentle strength – her body and soul laid bare in
this trusting fusion.

One powerful and enduring story about a female bear protecting a human is found in the mythology of the Ainu people, the indigenous people of Japan and Russia. The story is centered around the deity known as Korpokkur, a divine being associated with bears.

Long ago, there was a courageous Ainu hunter who wandered into the mountains in search of game and encountered a massive female bear. Instead of attacking the hunter, the bear approached him peacefully then transformed into a beautiful woman, revealing herself as Korpokkur.

Korpokkur spoke to the hunter, expressing her concern for the well-being of both bears and humans. She understood the necessity of hunting for survival but implored the hunter to treat the bears with respect and gratitude for the sustenance they provided.

To demonstrate her commitment to protecting humans, Korpokkur gifted the hunter with a magical bear claw. She explained that as long as he possessed the claw, no bear would harm him during his hunts. Grateful for her guidance and protection, the hunter returned to his village and shared the story of his encounter with the divine bear goddess.

From that day forward, the hunter became a respected figure in the Ainu community. He continued to hunt with reverence for the bears, always acknowledging the sacred connection between humans and these majestic animals.

This myth reflects the Ainu people's deep respect for nature, their understanding of the interconnectedness of all living beings, and the idea that divine entities, even in the form of bears, may serve as protectors and guides for those who approach the natural world with reverence.

Unguarded is an invitation to release the shields that protect you, to expose your true self without fear of judgment. In this vulnerability lies the potential for profound connection and transformation.

The powerful woman atop the bear represents a protective mother as they look after each other. Unguarded encourages you to embrace the maternal strength that lies within yourself and others. Like the bear, the protective mother supports, nurtures and defends, creating a safe space where vulnerability can coexist with supreme power.

Unguarded is an invitation to let yourself be loved and supported by people and situations that seem intimidating and fearful. There is a surprise harmonious connection to be experienced.

36 · Chalice of Charity

Be nourished

36 · Chalice of Charity

Be nourished

A woman's hand holds an upright chalice studded
with precious jewels as mystical spring water fountains
out in enchanting arcs. Her efforts are framed by
twigs woven into the inverted triangle creating
a sacred geometry aligned with the alchemical magic

of water – symbolizing fluidity, adaptability and emotional transformation.

Here is a promise of sustenance, abundance and replenishment. Water represents emotions and this cup offers sanctity and safe passage of these as the ability to go with the flow of life springs forth from this cup. Drink from it and there will be blessings of emotional momentum, getting past stuck feelings, old attitudes and trapped emotional states. This is the cup of plenty . . . plenty of love, plenty of gratitude, plenty of appreciation.

The chalice is a vessel of enchantment and emotional abundance replenishing your emotional reservoir and nurturing seeds of positivity within you. Be confident in the turn of events that are foretold when this card is drawn.

Like the Holy Grail of King Arthur's legend, Chalice of Charity serves as a supreme source of nourishment and sustenance by providing drink that never depletes, ensuring that those who partake in its offerings are always nourished.

If you have been feeling depleted and drained by concerns and fears, by situations that have not been what they promised, that have taken more than they have given, then nourishment and sustenance are now in your hands. And they can be relied upon to not be depleted until you have truly had your fill, for once the chalice is in your hands you will be called upon to offer it to others. The Chalice of Charity is not merely about material assistance but about fostering a sense of renewable and resilient sense of community, empathy and interconnectedness.

The greatest value of the Chalice of Charity is not the precious gems that stud its surface, nor the rare metal it is forged from, but the richness of the human spirit it contains. When you drink of this cup, the very best of what it is to be human shall be nourished.

About the author

Fiona Horne is one of the world's most respected witches. She is the author of 14 bestselling books on modern witchcraft, published over the last three decades, that see her work having a generational impact on the evolution of the modern witch. Her tireless devotion to dispelling negative myths and stereotypes has contributed to the freedom that modern witches have in practising their craft without fearing vilification and persecution.

Thirty years ago, Fiona launched a career in the entertainment industry as the lead singer of the chart-topping Aussie electro-rock band Def FX. In 1997 she released her first book, *Witch*, with Random House and became a popular radio and television personality, appearing on many programs globally.

Based in Los Angeles from 2001 to 2013, in addition to her many published books, Fiona scored prime-time

TV as 'The Witch' on SyFy channel's hit reality show *Mad Mad House* and was invited to speak at Harvard University on witchcraft in modern media.

Moving to the Caribbean in 2013, Fiona worked as a commercial pilot, public speaker and humanitarian/animal aid worker.

In 2017 she returned to publishing with her autobiography *The Naked Witch*, followed by 2019's manifesto *The Art of Witch* and 2021's *Teen Magick: Witchcraft for a New Generation*. Fiona also released her debut oracle deck *The Magick of You* to acclaim in 2019 followed by 2023's *Dark Magick Oracle*.

Fiona's personal passions include being a 100-foot-plus freediver, world record-holding skydiver, professional fire dancer and yoga instructor. She will always be a rockstar, as Def FX reunite for special tours and recently released a best of: *COLLECT Vol 1*.

In 2024 Fiona launched her 'Meet Yourself in . . .' nourishing spiritual adventures for women. Egypt, Bali and Kenya are her first offerings. To find out more visit Fiona's website:

FIONAHORNE.COM

 captainfifi

 fionahorneofficial

About the illustrator

Veronica Collins is an illustrator born and raised in Massachusetts where she lives with her husband and their dearly beloved black cat, Barnabas. Her hand is the creative force behind the works of Dark Solis. The influences that guide her creativity are born from her deep-rooted interest in old world witchery, paganism, occult history and mysterious folklore. Growing up in New England enriched her interest in history and folklore and she takes great inspiration from her surroundings. Veronica's illustrations come from a place of her own spiritualism as it  guides her musings and markings, her vision manifesting through her hands onto paper. The technique in which she is most proficient focuses on expressive line work and has gathered a reputation for being reminiscent of old woodcuts and etchings. Her work is constantly paying homage to the craft of artists such as Aubrey Beardsley,

Hans Holbein, Arthur Rackham, Alphonse Mucha, Rockwell Kent and Albrecht Dürer. Veronica's work makes nods to different eras of the past. She strives to capture the feeling of the old ways of a bygone age with a contemporary twist that is all her own.

Veronica has obtained a Bachelor in Fine Arts degree with a concentration in Illustration from the University of Massachusetts Dartmouth. Among her freelance work, she runs her own online shop selling her work in various forms under the name of Dark Solis.

To view more of her works visit:

DARKSOLIS.COM

darksolis.art